doll Parties

Celebrate with your doll all year long!

⭐ American Girl®

Published by American Girl Publishing, Inc.
Copyright © 2010 by American Girl, LLC

Questions or comments? Call 1-800-845-0005, visit our Web site at **americangirl.com**,
or write to Customer Service, American Girl, 8400 Fairway Place, Middleton, WI 53562-0497.

Printed in China
11 12 13 14 15 16 17 18 LEO 10 9 8 7 6 5 4 3

All American Girl marks are trademarks of American Girl, LLC.

Editorial Development: Trula Magruder

Art Direction & Design: Camela Decaire

Production: Jeannette Bailey, Sarah Boecher, Tami Kepler, Judith Lary

Photo Credit: Fireworks poster, © iStockphoto/ginosphotos

Set Photography: Travis Mancl & Greg Petz; Illustration: Casey Lukatz

Craft Stylist: Camela Decaire

Set Stylist: Jane Amini

Hand Model: Taylor M.

Craft with Care

When creating crafts or accessories that will touch your doll, remember
that dye colors from ribbons, felt, beads, and other supplies may bleed
color onto a doll and leave permanent stains. To help prevent this, use
light colors when possible, and check your doll often to make sure
colors aren't transferring to her body or vinyl. And never get your doll
wet! Water greatly increases the risk of dye rub-off.

Dear Doll Lover,

Celebrate special days in your doll's life with parties! This book shows four different kinds—a traditional birthday party, a Valentine's Day party, a costume party for Halloween, and a slumber party.

Throwing doll parties will be a piece of cake with the supplies and suggestions inside this kit. But don't stop with these ideas. As the party planner, you can add your own sweet touches. Wrap up pretend presents. Design goody bags. Plan great games. Serve tiny treats.

Remember: A doll party can be like any other party—only with smaller supplies . . . and shorter guests!

Your friends at
American Girl

Party Planning

Hosting a petite party will be simple with these supplies.

Itty Invitations

The mini invitations in your kit express your party theme. Pass out the invites to your friends or siblings for their dolls or stuffed animals.

Little "Linens"

Regular paper napkins can do double duty as doll-sized party linens. Completely unfold napkins for tablecloths, or cut tiny squares on the folds for dinner napkins.

Pint-Sized Plates

Jazz up your place settings with the paper plates in your kit. Use the plates to serve only pretend party treats. Do not eat real food off the plates.

Bitty Banners

Create excitement for your doll parties with the banners in your kit. To hang one, punch a hole on each side of the banner, slip strings through the holes, and tie the ends to a nearby object.

Cute Centerpieces

Bring whimsy to your party table with a colorful centerpiece. To make one, tape open the honeycomb base from your kit, and slip in a card cutout.

Wee Confetti

Sprinkle confetti on your party tables for sparkle. Buy small confetti, or use mini hole punches to make your own.

Sweet Streamers

Add tradition to your parties with streamers. Cut regular-size streamers into narrower strips. Lay the streamers on the party table, twist them around chair backs, or wrap them around the party cake. Note: Never hang streamers over lightbulbs, lamps, or other heat sources.

Darling Danglers

Display hanging decorations above party areas. Center the danglers over a decorated cardboard box, a card table, or a doll's table.

Bitty Rubber Bands

Help your doll get a grip! Slide a dowel rod or a lollipop stick inside a white or light-colored rubber band. Slip the rubber band over the back of a doll's hand as shown.

Birthday in Bloom

Tell your doll "I picked you" for a flower-filled birthday bash.

Blossom into Fun

The excitement for this petal party will grow when your doll's best "buds" open these invites. Pull out the invitations, fill them out, fold them along scored lines, and seal each one with a flower sticker.

Petal Party Hats

Pack personality into your party pics by dressing guests in matching hats from your kit. For each hat, attach double-stick tape along the edge marked "Tape here." Roll the hat into a cone until the side edges just overlap. Attach the hat with a plain bobby pin or the "Beauty Barrette" shown below.

Beauty Barrette

Make flattering flower barrettes for your guests. Cut a tiny leaf shape from green craft foam. Glue the leaf to the back edge of a flower-shaped shank button (the kind with a loop on the back). Let dry. Slide a pretty bobby pin through the shank.

Birthday!

Flower Favors

1. To make a doll lollipop, press a Glue Dot on the narrower end of a toothpick, and slip it inside a bead. Wrap a square piece of tissue paper around the bead.

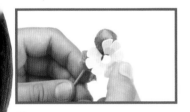

2. Pull out a flower collar from your kit, and slip it around the base of the bead. Make one for each guest.

Bitty Balloons

Brighten your party with colorful balloons. To make one, put a 4-inch Styrofoam "goose" egg in the center of tissue paper. Pull the paper up around the egg, gather it, and twist. Secure the tissue paper with a twist tie, and then cut off the extra paper with scissors. With an adult's help, carefully slide a skewer or dowel into the egg. Turn to page 5 to see how to attach the balloon to a doll's hand.

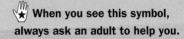

When you see this symbol, always ask an adult to help you.

Petite Party Cake

1. Decorate the cake box with some or all of the stickers included in your kit. Glue yarn either around the top edge or around both the top and bottom edges to look like icing.

2. For a pretend candle, glue on a pony bead as shown. Let dry. Cut a 1-inch piece from a stirrer straw, and slip it inside the bead. Push a paper flame into the tip of the straw.

Tip: If you want a different frosting, cover the cake with colored paper. Measure and cut out a paper circle for the top and a paper strip for the sides of the cake. Attach the paper cutouts with tape.

Pin the Petals

Help guests plant a garden in this game! With an adult's permission, tape the flower poster from your kit to a wall. Blindfold a doll, and help her attach a flower sticker to a stem.

Bitty Blindfolds

To blindfold a doll for party games, lay her down so that her eyes close, and then gently tie a ribbon around her head. (See "Craft with Care" on page 2 for dye cautions.)

✦ American Girl®

Tiny Valentine

Show your doll you have a big heart by throwing her a Valentine's Day party.

Have a Heart!

Each guest will open her heart to this sweet party. Pull out an invitation, and write a note on the right side of the blank heart. Fold the invite in half, and stick the bottom corners together with Glue Dots. Lift the heart flap to read the note. Repeat to invite more guests.

Happy Valentin

Heart Strings

Sweeten your doll's party scene with hanging hearts. Pull out the hearts from your kit, and tape them along pieces of pink embroidery floss. Hang the hearts near the party area.

Sugar "Cookies"

Make sweet valentine cookies. Use scissors or paper punches to cut craft foam into different-sized hearts. Layer the hearts as shown with craft glue. Glue a ribbon to the rim of a tin lid, let dry, and serve the pretend cookies.

Tiny Teddies

1. To make one of these favors, use craft glue to attach 2 medium-sized white pom-poms for feet to 1 extra-large white pom-pom for a body. Glue on a large white pom-pom for a head.

2. Glue on 4 small white pom-poms for front paws and ears. Attach black seed beads for the eyes and a nose. Dab glue on the edges of a craft-foam heart, and attach it to the bear's paws. Let dry.

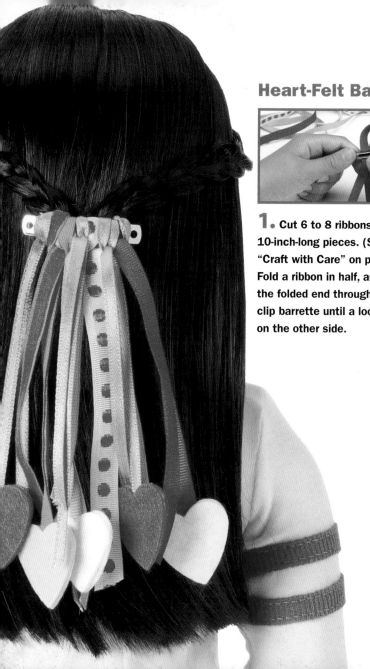

Heart-Felt Barrette

1. Cut 6 to 8 ribbons into 10-inch-long pieces. (See "Craft with Care" on page 2.) Fold a ribbon in half, and slip the folded end through a metal clip barrette until a loop shows on the other side.

2. Slip the ends of that same ribbon through the loop, and pull it tight to close the loop. Repeat with the other ribbons.

3. Press 2 self-stick heart-shaped felt pieces (available at craft stores) on opposite sides of a ribbon end. (For regular felt, use craft glue.) Repeat with a few more ends. Clip the barrette in the doll's hair.

All Heart

Before the party, use a paper punch to cut out a collection of hearts. Then ask an adult if it's OK to tape the hearts around the party area—on chair backs and walls or beneath plates. At some point, tell guests to quickly gather the hearts. Give a prize to the guest who collects the most hearts.

Designer Valentines

Create cute cards for party favors. Decorate folded squares of card stock with mini stickers. Give each doll a collection to keep or share.

Haunted Halloween

Scare up all of your doll's friends for a spooky shindig!

TO: Grace

HAPPY HALLOWEEN!
Join Taylor
Saturday at 4:00
Costumes
Ok!

Eek! Invitations

Set an eerie mood for this doll party with bat invites. Pull out the invitations, fill them out, and fold them along scored lines. Let guests know if they need to wear costumes.

Spooky Scene

Scare dolls stiff with these danglers. Punch out the spiders, webs, and bats. Use black thread to string them up near the party area.

Bat Mask

For a little mystery, mask your doll's face. Punch out the mask from your kit. Then cut two 12-inch-long pieces of ribbon. (See "Craft with Care" on page 2.) Knot the ends of the ribbons, and slip them through the mask holes so that the knots face out. Tie the other ends behind your doll's head.

Hair-Raising Accessories

For a spine-tingling style, place plastic spider rings into your doll's hair.

®/TM 2010 American Girl, LLC

Wicked Wings

1. Use pinking shears to cut black 100% cotton knit fabric into a 14-by-28-inch rectangle. (See "Craft with Care" on page 2.) Round the bottom corners with the shears.

2. Raise your doll's arms. Drape the fabric over her shoulders and arms so that the rounded corners are at the bottom. Then pull the fabric to her thumbs, and use chalk to mark thumb holes. Remove the fabric and snip a tiny cut at each mark. Insert the doll's thumbs into the holes.

Creepy "Candy"

Spread out a mix of Halloween treats. For a pretend candy bar, cut a 1½-by-1-inch piece of brown craft foam. Tape a candy wrapper from your kit around the foam piece. Repeat for more bars. Wrap beads in colorful foil and cellophane for pretend hard candies.

Note: Keep all pretend candies away from babies and small children.

Ghostly Giveaways

For a ghoulish favor, pass out pretend lollipop ghosts. Attach a Glue Dot to the narrower end of a toothpick, and slip it inside a bead hole. Drape a square of white tissue paper over the bead, and wrap on a mini rubber band or tie on a string. Add a ghost face with a marker.

Bone-Chilling Bingo

Pass out bingo cards and black buttons to guests. Then call out a B, I, N, G, or O and a picture shown on one of the cards (for example, "G pumpkin"). If a guest has the square you called, she covers it with a button. Call squares until someone fills a line down, across, or diagonally with buttons.

Starry Sleepover

Your doll will have stars in her eyes after this evening of entertainment.

Rise and Shine

Guests won't sleep a wink at this slumber party! Fill out the invitations, fold them in half along the scored lines, and hand them out to partygoers.

Swirly Curlies

1. Cut a ribbon so that it's 3 times longer than your doll's hair. Tie the middle of the ribbon around a small section of hair. Wrap both strands of ribbon around the hair section, and tie the ribbons in a knot.

2. Slip a star charm on the end of each ribbon strand. Tie a knot in each strand.

Night!

Super Stars

Guests can make wishes on these stars! Punch out the stars from your kit, and tape them along pieces of blue embroidery floss. Dangle the stars near the party area.

Sparkling "Cupcakes"

Surprise guests with these pretend "candy-coated" cupcakes. Place an extra-large white pom-pom in a mini cupcake liner. Use craft glue to attach seed beads and a rhinestone star to the pom-pom.

Shimmering Slippers

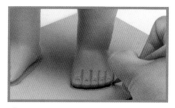

1. To make slipper soles, stand your doll on craft foam, and trace around her foot with a pencil. (See "Craft with Care" on page 2.) Cut out the soles with scissors. Using the soles as a pattern, make a second set.

2. Cut two 5-inch-long shiny ribbons for sandal straps. Holding a sole up to your doll's foot, wrap a ribbon around the foot and sole as shown. Attach the ribbon ends at the sole bottom with double-stick tape. Repeat for the other foot.

3. Glue the second set of soles to the first ones, covering the taped ribbons. Let dry. To decorate, glue small plain and sparkling pom-poms on the straps. Let dry.

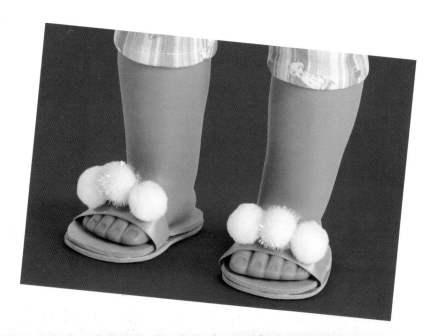

Party Puzzler

Gather guests and help them piece together a puzzle. To make it, glue the puzzle image from your kit on top of a thin piece of cardboard. Trim the cardboard, if needed. On the back of the puzzle, draw squiggly lines down and across. Cut along the lines with scissors. Mix the pieces up before putting the puzzle together.

Starburst Backdrop

 Turn dolls into superstars! With an adult's permission, tack or tape the fireworks poster from your kit to a wall. Pose the dolls in front of the poster for photos or performances.

Mini Microphone

Bring out a microphone for sing-alongs. To make a mic, attach a Glue Dot to the end of an oval tube bead. Slip a round bead over the oval bead and the Glue Dot. Tie or tape silver-colored string or floss to the oval bead.

Custom Karaoke

Get the party rockin' with your doll's very own boom box. To make the one in your kit, spread glue on the front and back flaps marked "Glue" before folding the box closed. Glue on the handle as shown. Let dry.

Signature Fun

Capture guests' "autographs" before they leave the party. To make the autograph book, punch out the pages from your kit, stack them so that the cover is on the outside, and staple the stack in the center. Fold the book closed. Ask partygoers to "sign" the book before they leave.

Autograph Here!

You shine!
Jenna

Thanks for the star treatment, Cassie!
Alex

Here are some other American Girl books you might like:

❑ *I read it.*

❑ *I read it.*

❑ *I read it.*

❑ *I read it.*

❑ *I read it.*